WHO CHANGED THE MESSAGE?

Remaining Faithful to Jesus's Call on Our Lives

Dr. Mario Elcock

sermonto**book**
.com

Sermon To Book
www.sermontobook.com

Who Changed the Message? Mario Elcock
ISBN-13: 978-1-945793-00-4
ISBN-10: 1-945793-00-7

Praise for
Who Changed the Message?

Dr. Elcock says it so well: "Once God redeems His people, there is a relationship and blessing to be found." He then leads the reader creatively and yet urgently to be faithful in not changing God's clear terms of embracing that relationship and blessing. *Who Changed The Message?* will challenge the reader to be steadfast in the things of God, knowing that it is His purposes that will ultimately prevail (Proverbs 19: 21). I highly recommend this book to all who are serious about remaining faithful to Jesus's call on their lives. Hopefully, reader, that represents your greatest desire. If it does, you will be encouraged as well as convicted, but most of all simply blessed as you mediate on the message contained here.

— *Pastor Stevan W. Ranson, B.Th., M.A. Hazelwood Christian Church, Clayton, Indiana*

What a timely piece of literature! Dr. Elcock has truly challenged this present-day generation of believers. This book is a must read! *Who Changed The Message?* ought to be in the hands of every believer. Once I started reading it, I couldn't put it down. It left me wanting more. I commend my brother for reminding us to remain faithful to the Master and the Message. Thank God for this passionate piece of writing.

— *Rev. Charles E. Adams, Jr., Pastor of Pilgrim Rest Missionary Baptist Church, Gary, Indiana*

Dr. Mario Elcock writes a relevant book on the matter of Salvation. He deals with the importance of the Christian believer to remain faithful and factual in the teaching and reaching of those who are lost. In this book, he emphasizes the universal need of salvation. He takes the reader on a journey from the Old Testament to the New Testament, to discover the Man, the Message, and the Method of this magnificent gift that God has given to all mankind: salvation!

— *Pastor Ronald Covington, Sr., Friendship Missionary Baptist Church, Indianapolis, Indiana*

As I look at the world around me, I am astounded at how timely *Who Changed the Message?* is in speaking to the needs of the human heart. In challenging popular notions of discipleship, evangelism, and baptism, the Reverend Dr. Mario Elcock offers a clarion call to all who claim the name Christian, and the heart of his message, though challenging, is one offered in love. My prayer is that all who read *Who Changed the Message?* will feel a renewed sense of calling and a claim on their lives to share the good news of Jesus Christ with a world in need.

— *Reverend Dustin Hite, Promise Road Campus Pastor, Geist Christian Church*

To my Lord and Savior, Jesus, the Christ: "For God so loved the world, that He gave His only begotten Son, that whoever believes in Him shall not perish, but have eternal life" (John 3:16 NASB). Thank You for loving me.

To my Love (Pretty Girl), my wife, who has collaborated with me in developing this book: You spent many nights with me after an exhausting day at work. Each moment we spend together is a time to cherish, and each expression of your love is a gift to treasure. You bring joy to my soul.

CONTENTS

Note from the Author

Thank you for purchasing *Who Changed the Message?*

Accompanying each main chapter of the book is a set of reflective questions with a practical, application-oriented action step. These workbook sections are a tool to help you understand the original, unchanging message of salvation found in God's Word.

I recommend you go through these workbook sections with a pen in order to write your thoughts and record notes in the areas provided. The questions are suitable for independent reflection, discussion with a friend, or review with a study group.

Regardless of what led you to this book or how you choose to approach it, I hope that the experience of reading and reflecting on it helps you put the real message of the gospel into practice as a present-day disciple of Jesus Christ.

—Dr. Mario Elcock

INTRODUCTION

Discipleship for a New Era

Bad theology is the main concern of this book. Somewhere along the line, people got involved in the gospel message—things were tweaked, theology was subtly adjusted, a division occurred, and the message got lost somewhere in church vision and mission statements. Now, people find themselves wading through mires of beliefs and doctrines that may or may not communicate what salvation really entails.

In this era of fast planes and moving trains, we must come to grips with the idea that the message of the gospel has not changed. In Matthew 28:19 we find The Great Commission, Jesus's last words to His disciples before leaving this earth to sit down at His father's right hand: "Go ye therefore, and teach all nations, baptizing them in the name of the Father, and of the Son, and of the Holy Ghost…"

This is the mandate established by Jesus Christ—the call on every person's life who confesses Jesus as Lord and Savior. Believers are called to help people come to a faith relationship with Him (evangelism), to commit to helping others learn and grow in their faith (discipleship), to connect them with other Christians in the local church so that their faith might be further built up (fellowship), to help people find their place in the ministry by discovering their spiritual gifts and then using them to edify the body of Christ (mission ministry), and finally, to lead people to express their adoration and love for God (worship).

My purpose in writing is to help equip those who have accepted the call to face the challenge of this new era, and to provide an opportunity for those who have not answered the call on their soul to do so. It is to help those who accept the call to clearly communicate the pure message of the gospel to others.

CHAPTER ONE

The Challenge of the Message

If it were Christ's intention to save all men, how deplorably He has been disappointed! — **Charles Spurgeon**[1]

Jesus made it clear that we must not only share the good news of the gospel of Christ with others, but we must also lead people to grow spiritually. We must model and instruct them in how to live in obedience to God's Word and follow Him. This is called discipleship, and should be the natural byproduct of those who follow Jesus. The message of salvation was not new to the New Testament followers of Jesus. The Sadducees, Pharisees, Zealots, and even the common Jewish people of the day held a messianic fervor that was the underlying purpose for their very existence. Their "savior" was everything they were waiting for—the person who would relieve them of Roman oppression, freeing them from their enemies.

To better understand where this concept of salvation came from, it is good to look back over biblical history to see that it was simply God's message from the beginning.

The Biblical Backdrop

In the Old Testament, a prominent theme runs through the Bible's pages. God, as Savior, is like a scarlet thread that starts in Genesis and winds its way through the Bible to the book of Revelation. The Hebrew word for salvation is *yeshuw'ah*. According to William Holladay, this word *yeshuw'ah* means, "help, prosperity or victory."[2]

In biblical redemptive history, *yeshuw'ah* referred to Israel's national salvation from foreign enemies, and also protection from those enemies. Additionally, it meant the individual salvation from the result of sin. Biblically, then, salvation alludes to deliverance from bondage and a new life of freedom. God is the superhero of this redemptive theme, the "*yeshuw'ah*" of man.

The first time this word "*yeshuw'ah*" was mentioned in the Old Testament was in Genesis 49:18. It reads, "I have waited for thy salvation (*yeshuw'ah*), O Lord." God's acts as *yeshuw'ah* are most vividly seen in the Exodus story. The Israelites are held captive in Egypt for almost four hundred years, but God in His faithfulness to His promises saved them from utter extinction by establishing a man named Moses to lead them from captivity to freedom.

Notice what Moses said to the Israelites about their soon-coming release from captivity: "Moses said unto the people, Fear ye not, stand still, and *see the salvation (yeshuw-ah) of the LORD*, which he will shew to you today: for the Egyptians whom ye have seen to day, ye shall see them again no more for ever" (Exodus 14:13, emphasis added).

Moses assures the people that God will be their Savior. Immediately after leading the Israelites through the Red Sea, bringing his people to safety, Moses sang a joyous praise song to the Israelites, saying: "The Lord is my strength and song, and he is become my salvation: he is my God, and I will prepare him an habitation; my father's God, and I will exalt him" (Exodus 15:2).

What a picture of what God does for us when we choose to put our faith in Him. He becomes our strength, song, and salvation.

King David also spoke of his relationship with God in terms of Salvation. The Psalms—many of which David wrote—speak of David's salvation from his enemies, Israel's deliverance as a nation, David's personal deliverance from his past sin with Bathsheba, and the wonder, expectation, and hope of a future salvation. Connecting this theme is that same term, *yeshuw'ah* (or a form of yeshuw'ah).

Take a look at Psalm 3:1-8, as one of many examples:

Lord, how are they increased that trouble me! many are they that rise up against me. Many there be which say of my soul, There is no help for him in God. Selah. But thou, O LORD, art a shield for me; my glory, and the lifter up of mine head. I cried unto the LORD with my voice, and he heard me out of his holy hill. Selah. I laid me down and slept; I awaked; for the LORD sustained me. I will not be afraid of ten thousands of people, that have set themselves against me round about. Arise, O LORD; save (yasha) me, O my God: for thou hast smitten all mine enemies upon the cheek bone; thou hast broken the teeth of the ungodly. Salvation (yeshuw-ah) belongeth unto the LORD: thy blessing is upon thy people. Selah.

In both examples above, nothing was required of Moses or David but belief—having faith in the God of salvation. The writer of 2 Chronicles 20:17 affirms this concept of salvation through faith: "Ye shall not need to fight in this battle: set yourselves, stand ye still, and see the salvation of the Lord with you, O Judah and Jerusalem: fear not, nor be dismayed; to morrow go out against them: for the LORD will be with you." *Stand, and see.*

The exodus out of Egypt was much more than a release from oppression, and David's praise of national and personal salvation was more than a one-time "freedom."

In his book *Far as the Curse Is Found*, Michael D. Williams said the following:

The initial act of physical deliverance is just that, initial. More is to come. For all believers, salvation is more than deliverance from the oppression of sin, guilt, and death. God wants not only to save but also to enter into a relationship with His covenant community and to bless that community. Relationship and blessing lay alongside deliverance at the heart of redemption.[3]

Salvation is the main theme of Christianity. It is the good news portrayed through the Word of God. Salvation expresses the idea of rescue from jeopardy and misery into a state of safety. But it is not the end-all. Once God redeems His people, there is a relationship and blessing to be found. This is where *discipleship* comes in, where believers must encourage each other to "work out your own salvation with fear and trembling" (Philippians 2:12).

Against this biblical and historical backdrop, then, we must ask ourselves: Has the message of salvation changed? There seems to have evolved a slight hiccup in this plan to disciple the world. The message—the good news of the gospel of salvation—seems to have been altered.

For some Christians, salvation beliefs according to the Word of God have evolved to express different meanings. Let's begin to answer this question by examining the differing beliefs of three modern-day denominations: the Congregational Church, the Church of Christ, and the Baptist Church. Doing so will help us see if there is anything different in understanding how people are changed from God's enemies to His friends. The results of what we find could make a huge difference in what is communicated to not-yet-believers regarding salvation.

How Has the Message Changed?

One of the main differences in views is regarding the relationship between baptism and salvation. The Congregational Church and Baptist Church do not believe baptism is essential for salvation. These denominations see baptism as a response toward obedience, but not a necessity. The Baptist Church says that when people come to Jesus Christ for salvation, they enter into an undiscoverable union with Him, so that what happened to Christ happened to us. Christ dies, therefore, we die; Christ rose, and therefore, we are raised with Him. Christ ascended, and we ascended with Him. They use Paul's words, "I am crucified with Christ: nevertheless I live; yet not I, but Christ liveth in me: and the life which I now live in the flesh I live by the faith of the Son of God, who loved me, and gave himself for me" (Galatians 2:20) as biblical evidence for this belief.

But before I entertain the contrast in belief, let me say that there are some similarities. The sacred text used in all three denominations is the Holy Bible. All three also see the Trinity as the eternal tribune in whom God reveals Himself to us as the Father, Son, and Holy Spirit, with distinct personal attributes, but without division of nature, essence, or being. Yet another similarity is that these churches do not have an age restriction on membership but will not accept a child as a member, who is considered too young to fully understand and make a profession of faith of their own volition and comprehension.

The common belief in the resurrection of Christ is also quite evident in each of these denominations: Christ died, was buried, and was resurrected by God for all who believe in Him. This resurrection is God's most amazing miracle and proof that Jesus was indeed divine.

Despite these similarities, there are many differences between the Congregational Church, Church of Christ, and the Baptist Church, as I have discovered by attending services at all three types of churches. Not all of these differences, however, are apparent at first glance. Many of these differences have more to do with root theological religious differences between all three denominations—differences in appearances between the church buildings. (Theology, by the way, means the "study of God.") Let's look at these differences.

The Congregational Church's Understanding of Salvation

In the Congregational Church, it is their belief that "God promises forgiveness and grace to save us from sin and shamelessness to all who trust Him, who accept His call to serve the whole human family."

Congregational churches are Protestant Christian churches practicing congregational church government in which each congregation independently runs its own affairs. Many Congregational churches claim their descent from the original Congregational churches, a family of Protestant denominations with a formal theory of union published by the theologian Robert Browne in

1592. The church of Christ denomination believes, "A person must hear the gospel and believe in Christ, repent, confess Christ, be baptized, and persevere in holiness to be saved."

For the past forty years within the Congregational Church (Presbyterian), there has been some controversy because of this denomination's belief about how people are saved. Their membership has declined by about fifty thousand a year, and a new crisis has developed within the church over belief and practices as some conservative members believe the loss is related to the church's continuation for many decades of the decision to provide equal rights for gays and lesbians.

The controversy originated in the question of salvation for homosexuals and the question of whether to ordain such persons for ministry. Especially from the late 1990s onward, however, the arguments have turned toward recognition of holy unions for committed same-sex couples and the question of whether a path exists for personal salvation apart from belief in Jesus. Yet with regard to the latter, we read in Scripture:

> *I am crucified with Christ: nevertheless I live; yet not I, but Christ liveth in me: and the life which I now live in the flesh I live by the faith of the Son of God, who loved me, and gave himself for me.*— **Galatians 2:20**

An article in the *Informer* by Nathaniel Boyd, Sr., said, "Christian education must start in the home first and then expand into the communities."[4] He cites a verse in Hosea 4:6, "My people are destroyed for lack of knowledge: because thou hast rejected knowledge, I will also reject thee." If we do not teach our children according to God's Word, the streets will teach them how not to follow Christ. *Who changed the message?*

The Church of Christ's Understanding of Salvation

In 1997, preachers from the Church of Christ and Pastor David Martin of Solid Rock Baptist Church engaged in a debate over the subject of their salvation beliefs. There were 250 people who attended this debate.[5]

The Church of Christ believes you must be baptized for your salvation. David Martin asked their preachers several questions: If a Church of Christ elder refuses to baptize me, will I be lost until I can find one who will? Do I need Jesus and a Campbellite preacher in order to be saved? If I do, then Jesus Christ is not the only mediator of salvation, contrary to 1 Timothy 2:5—"For there is one God, and one mediator between God and men, the man Christ Jesus..." Moreover, if such is the case, then the Holy Spirit is not the only administrator of salvation, which contradicts 1 Corinthians 12:13—"For by one Spirit are we all baptized into one body, whether we be Jews or Gentiles, whether we be bond or free; and have been all made to drink into one Spirit."

The Church of Christ preacher is thus necessary for salvation, for he is performing a saving act on the person when he baptizes them. Is this not blasphemy against Jesus Christ and the Holy Spirit?

David Martin concluded by asking, "If the water pipes and the baptistery was bone dry, would my salvation have to wait until a plumber showed up? If I were to die before then, would I go to hell? Obedience to water baptism is the means of forgiveness of sins."

The Church of Christ teaches that a sinner is forgiven from sin when a capable elder baptizes him in water. Pastor Martin declared, "Where does the Bible teach that water baptism is required in order to have one's sins forgiven? Every time the phrase "for the remission of sin" occurs it is speaking of the fact that sins have been forgiven previously.

The Baptist Understanding of Salvation

In the Baptist community, by contrast, the main theme of the gospel is salvation. Salvation is a picture-word of wide application that expresses the idea of rescue from jeopardy and misery into a state of safety.

Moses and the sons of Israel declared this in Exodus 15:2, singing, "The LORD is my strength and song, and he is become my salvation: he is my God, and I will prepare him an habitation; my father's God, and I will exalt him." Jonah said, "I am an Hebrew; and I fear the LORD, the God of heaven, which hath made the sea and the dry land" (Jonah 1:9). The psalmist proclaimed, "The Lord preserveth the simple: I was brought low, and he helped me" (Psalm 116:6). And after being shipwrecked on Malta, Paul said, "Wherefore I pray you to take some meat: for this is for your health: for there shall not an hair fall from the head of any of you" (Acts 27:34).

The gospel proclaims that the same God who saved Israel from Egypt, Jonah from the fish's belly, the psalmist from death, and soldiers from drowning also saves people today. This same God saves all who have put their trust in Christ from their sin and sin's consequences.

In his book on purpose-driven discipleship, Tom Holladay wrote that the Baptist view regards the Bible as the authority shaping a person's life. Yet predictably, given the name of their denomination, Holladay sees baptism to be a potential distraction for Baptists, including in their insistence on believers' baptism and rejection of infant baptism. As Holladay explained:

> Baptists consider Christian baptism to be an ordinance for believers only, by emersion only, and as a symbolic act, not having power in itself. The act of baptism pictures what Christ has done for the believers in his death, burial, and resurrection?[6]

The Bible plainly teaches that the forgiveness of sin is conditioned upon repentance of sin and faith in Christ—never upon baptism. John the Baptist said in Matthew 3:11, "I indeed baptize you with water unto repentance: but he that cometh after me is mightier than I, whose shoes I am not worthy to bear: he shall baptize you with the Holy Ghost, and with fire…"

Moreover, when Christ made the statement, "For this is my blood of the new testament, which is shed for many for the remission of sins" (Matthew 26:28), He was indicating that remission of sin did not occur at baptism. Rather, Jesus came to take away sins to redeem us and pay the sin debt with His own precious blood. Clearly, repentant, believing sinners had been forgiven all through the Old Testament, and Christ shed His blood because God forgave these believers for thousands of years before Jesus's crucifixion and resurrection.

If salvation is not by works of righteousness, then how can water baptism be a part of salvation in the Bible? We are saved by grace, and grace does not involve human effort or merit. Grace is grace, and works are works, as Paul taught, saying, "For by grace are ye saved through faith; and that not of yourselves: it is the gift of God: Not of works, lest any man should boast" (Ephesians 2:8-9).

The Baptist adheres to the belief that while humanity is fallen, Christ came to pay the penalty for our sins on the cross. This is good news. That penalty, now paid in full, means God offers forgiveness and new life as a free gift. All who have received Christ as Lord may have it. Baptists do not believe that true believers will fall away, and thereby lose their salvation. This is sometimes called "once saved, always saved." The proper term, however, is "the final perseverance of the saints." It means real Christians stick with it. It doesn't mean believers won't stumble, but refers to an inward pull that will not allow them to quit the faith.

The Baptist further believes that when one receives Jesus Christ as Lord, the Holy Spirit does an internal work within that person to redirect his or her life, making him or her to be born again—the biblical term for which is "regeneration." This is not merely choosing to turn over a new leaf, but is also a matter of God beginning a lifelong process of changing our desires and affections. The only way to get into heaven is salvation through Jesus Christ. In Romans 10:9, Paul said, "That if thou shall confess with thy mouth the Lord Jesus, and shalt believe in thine heart that God hath raised him from the dead, thou shalt be saved."

The Baptist profile of Jesus Christ through salvation is Jesus of Nazareth. He is the Christ—the Anointed One, or the Messiah. The name Jesus is derived from *yeshuh-ah*, that same Hebrew-Aramaic word used throughout the Old Testament, meaning, "Yahweh (the Lord) is salvation." The name Christ is actually a title for Jesus. It comes from the Greek word *Christo*, meaning "the Anointed One."

Thus, Jesus, who is God in the flesh, is named "the Lord is salvation." How fitting—His name is salvation, and He did save, indeed.

WORKBOOK

Chapter 1 Questions

Question: What are some of the different versions of God's message that people believe?

_____

_____

_____

_____

_____

_____

_____

_____

_____

_____

Question: What is the biblical message? How do we know?

_____

_____

_____

_____

_____

_____

_____

_____

_____

_____

_____

_____

Question: What is the role of baptism in biblically based Christian practice?

_____

_____

_____

_____

_____

_____

_____

_____

_____

_____

Action: Study the biblical message of salvation, and beware the changes and distractions that various doctrines try to add to God's Word. Do not replace the grace of God with baptism, works of righteousness, or equal rights at the center of your faith. Rather, let acts and works flow from the transformation that God's grace brings to your life.

Chapter 1 Notes

_____

_____

_____

_____

_____

_____

_____

_____

_____

_____

_____

_____

_____

_____

_____

_____

_____

_____

_____

_____

_____

_____

CHAPTER TWO

A Saving Faith

If in preaching the gospel you substitute your knowledge of the way of salvation for confidence in the power of the gospel, you hinder people from getting to reality. — **Oswald Chambers**[7]

The debate on salvation and how humanity achieves eternal life will continue until the Second Coming of Christ. Yet I must confess, I am biased in my writing. I must hold to my faith. I believe in the death, burial, and resurrection of Jesus Christ, and anyone who confesses with their mouth and believes in their heart that God raised Him from the grave shall be saved from the pits of hell and be with Jesus in heaven. The famous passage in Hebrews 11, sometimes called the Hall of Faith, lists characters in both the Old and New Testaments who were saved; clearly, people were saved before the crucifixion of Christ, and before baptism.

Some of the great Old Testament saints listed in Hebrews 11 are Isaac, Jacob, Joseph, Moses, David, and the Father of faith—Abraham. Through faith, they conquered kingdoms, administered justice, obtained promises, shut mouths of lions, quenched raging fires, escaped the edge of the sword, won strength out of weakness, became mighty in war, and put foreign armies to flight. Let's look at one set of verses from Hebrews 11:

> *By faith Abraham, when he was called to go out into a place which he should after receive for an inheritance, obeyed; and he went out, not knowing whither he went. By faith he sojourned in the land of promise, as in a strange country, dwelling in tabernacles with Isaac and Jacob, the heirs with him of the same promise: For he looked for a city which hath foundations, whose builder and maker is God. Through faith also Sara herself received strength to conceive seed, and was delivered of a child when she was past age, because she judged him faithful who had promised. Therefore sprang there even of one, and him as good as dead, so many as the stars of the sky in multitude, and as the sand which is by the sea shore innumerable. These all died in faith, not having received the promises, but having seen them afar off, and were persuaded of them, and embraced them, and confessed that they were strangers and pilgrims on the earth.*— **Hebrews 11:8-13**

If Hebrews 11 lists these men and women as saints, then they must have been saved. But the question is: *how* were they saved, if Jesus Himself said in John 14:6, "*I am* the way and the truth and the life. No one comes to the Father except through me" (John 14:6 NIV, emphasis added)? One couldn't have been baptized in the name of

Jesus in Old Testament times because He hadn't even been born yet.

There must have been something different than baptism that saves.

Belief in the Promise to Come

Let's look at a promise God made to Abraham (also known as "Abram" in the Old Testament):

> *Now the LORD had said unto Abram, Get thee out of thy country, and from thy kindred, and from thy father's house, unto a land that I will shew thee: And I will make of thee a great nation, and I will bless thee, and make thy name great; and thou shalt be a blessing: And I will bless them that bless thee, and curse him that curseth thee: and in thee shall all families of the earth be blessed.* — **Genesis 12:1-3**

God promised a Savior who would come through one of Abraham's descendants. This Savior would bless all families of the earth. We know this to be none other than Jesus Christ, the Messiah. However, Abraham had never heard of Jesus and the necessity of believing in His life, death, and resurrection for salvation. How, then, was he saved? A few chapters later in Genesis 15:6, we are given the answer: "And he [Abram] believed in the LORD; and he counted it to him for righteousness."

The last verse in the scripture above says that Abraham believed God's promise that he would have a descendant.

Of course, Abraham and every person on earth who existed prior to the cross did not know Jesus—or even about Him. But Scripture says that their belief was credited to them as righteousness. This means that their faith in the promise to come saved them.

Old Testament saints believed in the promise God had made of a redeemer who would save them from sin—and they always knew that redeemer to be God Himself. Consider the following three verses—written hundreds of years before Jesus was even born:

I, even I, am the LORD; and beside me there is no saviour.
— Isaiah 43:11

Salvation belongeth unto the LORD: thy blessing is upon thy people **— Psalm 3:8**

The LORD is my strength and song, and is become my salvation. **— Psalm 118:14**

When Jesus arrived, God made good on His promise to Adam, Eve, Abraham, Isaac, Jacob, and every person who believed what God said prior to the cross. They were saved by their faith, not by baptism—or any other good work. This is why Paul was able to say with confidence, "For by grace are ye saved through faith; and that not of yourselves: it is the gift of God: Not of works, lest any man should boast" (Ephesians 2:8-9).

Old Testament saints looked forward to the cross and believed God for what He would do. New Testament saints looked back and continue to look back to the cross and believe what He did. Old Testament and New Testament saints were and are saved the same way: *by faith.*

For Him or Against Him?

What exactly is faith? *Webster's New World College Dictionary* defines faith as "unquestioning belief that does not require proof or evidence; unquestioning belief in God, religious tenets."[8] Though it's a good definition, let's consider a biblical alternative.

Hebrews 11:1 says faith is "the substance of things hoped for, the evidence of things not seen." The irony in life is that man has tremendous amounts of faith in what he can do, but little faith, most of the time, in what God can do.

> *But without faith it is impossible to please him: for he that cometh to God must believe that he is, and that he is a rewarder of them that diligently seek him.* — *Hebrews 11:6*

The writer of Hebrews 11:6 said there are two key elements to faith: Belief in God, and belief that He will be the one to reward—to meet the deepest needs of a person's soul. Notice, too, that without faith, it is impossible to please God. Without faith, a person stands against God.

Faith in Action

There is a beautiful example of faith in action in the New Testament. In Matthew 9:27-30, two blind men came to Jesus, begging for Him to give them sight. Jesus first asked, "Believe ye that I am able to do this?" Both men answered, "Yes!" Jesus touched their eyes, and told them, "...according to your faith be it unto you." Their faith had healed them; their eyes were opened. Their faith, the assurance Jesus could open their blind eyes, was the substance of the reality they hoped for. It was also the evidence that they would receive what they had asked for.

Another example of great faith involved three men in the book of Daniel: Shadrach, Meshach, and Abed-nego. These men—Daniel's friends—refused to bow to King Nebuchadnezzar's gold image:

> *If it be so, our God whom we serve is able to deliver us from the furnace of blazing fire; and He will deliver us out of your hand, O king. But even if He does not, let it be known to you, O king, that we are not going to serve your gods or worship the golden image that you have set up.—* ***Daniel 3:17-18 (NASB)***

All three were thrown into a fiery furnace and should have died instantly. Certainly they had no idea what would happen to them for coming against the king. Their faith, like that of the two blind men, was in the substance of what they hoped for—God's promises in His Word— and it was the evidence of that which had not yet been seen or received. Their faith was founded on serving God and obeying Him—to the point of death. They believed God would deliver, based on the promises God had declared in His word.

Conversely, a lack of faith will have obvious results. When the disciples were unable to heal a man with a demon, they asked Jesus, "Why could not we cast him out?"(Matthew 17:19).

Jesus responded, "Because of your unbelief." He then went on to say, "If ye have faith as a grain of mustard seed, ye shall say unto this mountain, Remove hence to yonder place; and it shall remove; and nothing shall be impossible unto you" (Matthew 17:20).

If the disciples could not cast the demons out without faith, how can we as followers of Jesus expect hearts to be transformed simply by our words? We must have faith that Jesus will be the one to save; we must only believe, and walk in obedience. We must speak when He says speak, love when He says love, and be silent when He says to be silent. Trust Him to do the work of salvation.

Coming to a Saving Faith

Strength of my heart, I need not fail,
Not mind to fear but to obey,
With such a Leader, who could quail?
Thou art as Thou wert yesterday.
Strength of my heart, I rest in Thee,
Fulfill Thy purposes through me.

—Amy Carmichael[9]

For a person to come to a saving faith, there must be more than a mere acceptance of something as true. Rather, a saving faith involves trust—a reliance on that something. In the case of salvation, it requires reliance on Christ.

The Protestant Reformers of the sixteenth and seventeenth centuries approached faith in three ways, or considered faith as having three aspects: knowledge, assent, and trust. David Reagan of Lamband Lion Ministries explains these three aspects as follows:[10]

Knowledge

Faith begins with a knowledge of what it is that should be believed. For instance, if someone knows the gospel of Christ refers to the death, burial, and resurrection of Christ according to the Scriptures, they have knowledge. However, it is possible for someone to know what the gospel is and still not believe it is truth. This is true of many atheists today. In this case, knowledge is clearly not enough.

Belief (Assent)

Because knowledge is not enough, the person must also believe that the object of faith is true. To reach this level of faith, the person must know what the gospel is— knowledge—and believe it to be true—assent. But this is still not enough for salvation. There is a third and very important aspect of faith.

Trust

Trust refers to a personal commitment to and reliance upon the object of faith. In salvation, the object of faith is Jesus. The sinner must know Jesus died for him and rose again from the dead—knowledge. Next, he must accept these facts are true—assent. However, he is still not saved until he relies on these facts as the basis for his personal salvation. Let me give you a couple of illustrations to help you understand these three aspects.

Let's create a scenario. Say you are visiting a friend's home and they ask you to sit down. First, you look over and acknowledge that there is indeed a chair. This is knowledge. Next, you accept the fact you could sit in this chair and it would hold you up. That is assent. Finally, you walk over to the chair and sit down in it. That is trust.

It is in this third aspect of faith—trusting God—that the believer exercises and completes faith. This is what the psalmist communicated in Psalm 28:7: "The LORD is my strength and my shield; my heart trusted in him, and I am helped: therefore my heart greatly rejoiceth; and with my song will I praise him."

This, too, is why discipleship is so important. Followers of Jesus have a call on their lives to share the good news of the gospel and "make disciples of all nations, baptizing them in the name of the Father, and of the Son, and of the Holy Ghost..."

WORKBOOK

Chapter 2 Questions

Question: How were believers saved before the ministry, crucifixion, and resurrection of Christ? What significance does this hold for us today?

_____

_____

_____

_____

_____

_____

_____

_____

_____

_____

_____

Question: Why and how, specifically, should you put your faith into action in your daily life?

_____
_____
_____
_____
_____
_____
_____
_____
_____
_____
_____

Question: What does having a saving faith require?

_____
_____
_____
_____
_____
_____
_____
_____
_____
_____
_____

Action: Know that faith in God's love, sacrifice, and mercy saves! Believe this in your heart; and trust in your faith in God's grace to save you. Read in the Bible about the saints of the Old Testament whose faith alone saved them; yet also put your faith into practice as they did.

Chapter 2 Notes

CHAPTER THREE

Evangelism: Leading People to Faith

As soon as a man has found Christ, he begins to find others. — **Charles Spurgeon**[11]

Every person is created with a spiritual vacuum that will be filled by something—either divine spiritual truth or demonic spiritual lies. People have an innate desire to be changed in a way that will make them feel less guilty and more content. They will fill this need by immersing themselves in different programs, philosophies, and religions—but unless they are filled with Jesus, this will be for nothing.

In the era in which we live, we must lead people to a belief and greater faith in Jesus Christ. This involves sharing the gospel—the good news about Jesus Christ, who fills the hole in us. God's greatest desire is to spend eternity with those He created and loves. But this will never happen unless we—God's people—get the message out.

This is what evangelism is: to share with others that Jesus Christ died on a cross for the sins of all mankind and rose again on the third day. Ever since Jesus declared what we know as the Great Commission—to go into the entire world and preach the gospel to every creature—Christians have been busy doing the ministry of evangelism.

There are many different approaches and techniques, many how-to books, and even classes one can take to become skilled in winning people for Christ. But are we, in this generation, presenting the real message of who Jesus is? Are we telling people the right thing?

Why People Struggle to Evangelize

Before we look at the message of salvation, let's consider reasons why people struggle to evangelize.

Fear

Sharing with others about who Jesus is and what He has done for them can sometimes be scary. In fact, this is the number one reason why people don't share their faith. There is no special trick or technique that will make it any less scary, but there is comfort in knowing that if God has commanded it, He won't leave His people alone to do it. God desires that none should perish but all should come to repentance (2 Peter 3:9), and because of that, you can come to Him with every concern you have—including the fact that you are afraid. Ask God to guide you toward opportunities to share your faith and to remove any fear you have. And remember: nothing you do will be able to save someone; the message of the cross is what has the power to save (1 Corinthians 1:18).

Ignorance

Many followers of Jesus want to share their faith, but have no idea where to start or what to say. And many Christians aren't even aware that they have been called to proclaim the gospel at all. If this is you, you are not alone. However, don't let ignorance stop you anymore. Paul wrote in 1 Corinthians 15:3-4, "For I delivered unto you first of all that which I also received, how that Christ died for our sins according to the scriptures; And that he was buried, and that he rose again the third day according to the scriptures." This is the gospel. You have it in a nutshell and are no longer in a place of ignorance.

Arrogance

Some people, though it may be subconscious, think they are above sharing the gospel. Or they believe this job is set aside for pastors or missionaries. John Piper, a popular Christian writer and speaker, said:

> Evangelism can never be finished, but missions can be finished. The reason is this: Missions have the unique task of crossing language and culture barriers to penetrate a people group and establish a church movement, but evangelism is the ongoing task of sharing the gospel among people within the same culture.[12]

Paul said in Romans 3:23 (NIV), "all have sinned and fall short…" of God's glory. This means parents and children—even best friends or the cranky neighbor down the street. Everyone needs to hear the good news of salvation. You may be the only person who shares the gospel with certain people in your circle of influence.

The ministry of evangelism is set aside for no one. If you are a believer in Christ, you are to share the gospel. Period.

Apathy

Some people simply don't give a second thought to the lost. Or they only care about those who are closest to them—family, friends, or people they are comfortable with. But outside of their circle of influence, it doesn't even cross their mind that every lost person at the supermarket, every unsaved parent of a child on a sports team, every person at the gym who does not know Jesus is someone you may be called to share the gospel with. God is no respecter of persons, and we should not be either. Matthew says,

Therefore everyone who confesses Me before men, I will also confess him before My Father who is in heaven. But whoever denies Me before men, I will also deny him before My Father who is in heaven.— **Matthew 10:32-33 (NASB)**

Jesus made it clear: Sharing the good news should always be on the believer's mind. We are to confess Christ before men. To choose otherwise is to deny Him.

The True Message of Salvation

It is of utmost importance for the person sharing the gospel with another person, or later discipling a person, to have a sound theological foundation themselves. And it is not difficult. However, it may take some effort to make sure you understand the message of salvation yourself before you try to communicate it to others.

Repentance

An excellent biblical place to start is the same place John the Baptist started: with repentance. In fact, this message was not new. For centuries, prophet after prophet had been calling Israel to repent for her wicked deeds and turn back to God. Consider the following three verses:

If you will return, O Israel, says the LORD, return unto me: and if you will put away your abominations out of my sight, then shall you not be moved. — **Jeremiah 4:1**

> *Therefore also now, saith the Lord, turn ye even to me with
> all your heart, and with fasting, and with weeping, and with
> mourning...* — ***Joel 2:12***

> *Therefore say thou unto them, Thus saith the LORD of
> hosts; Turn ye unto me, saith the LORD of hosts, and I will
> turn unto you, saith the LORD of hosts.* — ***Zechariah 1:3***

Then John the Baptist came on the scene. And what was his message? Pretty much the same as the prophets before him. John said, "Repent, for the kingdom of heaven is at hand!"(Matthew 3:2 NKJV). And lest you think Jesus taught anything different, His message echoes both John and the prophets. Matthew 4:17 (NKJV) says, "From that time Jesus began to preach, and to say, 'Repent, for the kingdom of heaven is at hand.'" Yes, repentance was at the center of Jesus's message, and is paramount for salvation.

Repentance involves a change of heart or a change of mind. Paul said in 2 Corinthians 7:10 that repentance also includes sorrow for past offenses: "For godly sorrow worketh repentance to salvation not to be repented of: but the sorrow of the world worketh death"—as well as an understanding of and grievance for the personal sin and evil committed against God. The Psalmist affirms this, saying, "Against thee, thee only, have I sinned, and done this evil in thy sight: that thou mightest be justified when thou speakest, and be clear when thou judgest" (Psalm 51:4).

The Bad News

Man is separated from God, who is holy, righteous, and cannot look upon sin. God literally hates sin. The Bible says He is "angry with the wicked every day" (Psalm 7:11). Because of this, all human beings stand in judgment before God and are incapable of doing anything about the situation.

Without God, people are in a state of sin against Him, and because of this, death—eternal separation from God—and judgment is unavoidable (Hebrews 9:27). Hebrews 10:11 also says, "And every priest standeth daily ministering and offering oftentimes the same sacrifices, which can never take away sins..." The priests in the Old Testament couldn't permanently take away sin, and neither can man. There is nothing a person can do in and of him- or herself to fix the situation.

The Good News!

But with God—who is holy, loving, forgiving to a thousand generations, and the very creator of salvation—there is hope. There is good news. This is called the gospel. The word gospel actually means "good news." This is the next step in the message of salvation—communicating that even though there is sin, there is also hope. God provided a perfect sacrifice for sin, because of His love and mercy toward His children whom He loves. Salvation is a gift from the Lord, and nothing man can obtain on his own, as the apostle Paul wrote: "For by grace are ye saved through faith; and that not of yourselves: it is the gift of God: Not of works, lest any man should boast" (Ephesians 2:8-9).

Confess and Believe

The Bible says that to obtain salvation, we are to confess Jesus with our mouth and believe He is Lord over the entire world. Nothing more. "That if thou shalt confess with thy mouth the Lord Jesus, and shalt believe in thine heart that God hath raised him from the dead, thou shalt be saved" (Romans 10:9).

What does a person need to accept? They need to accept the sacrifice that was made for them to remedy the dire situation they are in. If they confess their sins to God and repent—or turn away—from their sins, they will be saved. There is no long list of good deeds to do that will make a person savable. No, one must only believe.

This full picture must be presented before the good news can be received.

Evangelism Is Not a Sales Pitch

Paul said in Romans 1:16 that he was not ashamed of the gospel, and we should not be ashamed either. Evangelism is not a sales pitch, but rather telling people the truth. Someday, Jesus will return to judge the living and the dead. On that day, all who believe in him will join God in the new creation—a creation forever free from sin, sadness, and death. We tell people how their relationship with God can be restored to how it was supposed to be; we don't want people to experience eternal separation from God, wrath, judgment, and hell. Therefore, telling people about Jesus is one of the most powerful acts of love anyone can ever extend to another person.

From that point on, followers of Jesus should go forward, obey His Word—the Bible—and begin sharing the good news with others.

How to Naturally Share the Gospel

> It seems that invariably, when someone becomes a true follower of Christ, that person's first impulse is to want to find a friend and introduce that friend to Christ. — **John MacArthur**[13]

The easiest way to start talking about Jesus, especially for those who are hesitant about sharing the gospel, is to ask questions. People will be more interested in hearing what you have to say once you have listened to what they have to say first. It also allows you to know where they are spiritually, to better gauge how to talk to them. Some questions you can ask include:

- Do you have any kind of spiritual beliefs?
- Did you grow up in a home that practiced any kind of religion, or went to church?
- Who is Jesus to you?
- If you died tonight, where do you think you would go?
- If what you believe at this moment about God were not true, would you want someone to tell you?

Questions like these will help naturally move a conversation from worldly, secular talk to a meaningful spiritual discussion.

Ultimately, you will want to let God's Word do the "speaking" for you. Again, there is nothing YOU can do in and of yourself to make a person believe in Jesus. The following are just a few verses you can memorize and then share with friends during these natural conversations. God's Word is sharper than any double-edged sword (Hebrews 4:12); trust it to do the work for you.

For all have sinned and fall short of the glory of God.— **Romans 3:23 (NIV)**

For the wages of sin is death, but the gift of God is eternal life in Christ Jesus our Lord.— **Romans 6:23 (NIV)**

In reply, Jesus said, "Very truly I tell you, no one can see the kingdom of God unless they are born again" (John 3:3 NIV). Then, again, in John 14:6 (NIV): "Jesus answered, 'I am the way and the truth and the life. No one comes to the Father except through me.'"

Consider Romans 10:9-11 (NIV), which says,

If you declare with your mouth, "Jesus is Lord," and believe in your heart that God raised him from the dead, you will be saved. For it is with your heart that you believe and are justified, and it is with your mouth that you profess your faith and are saved. As Scripture says, "Anyone who believes in him will never be put to shame."

Then in 2 Corinthians 5:15 (NIV), Scripture says, "And he died for all, that those who live should no longer live for themselves but for him who died for them and was raised again."

The Christian should not be afraid of sharing the gospel. It is the good news unto salvation. Ask the Lord to help you overcome your concerns, and He will direct your paths.

Chapter 3 Questions

Question: Why do people struggle to evangelize? What about evangelism represents a challenge or struggle for you personally, and how can you overcome this hang-up?

_____

_____

_____

_____

_____

_____

_____

_____

_____

_____

Question: What exactly is the message we need to share?

_____

_____

_____

_____

_____

_____

_____

_____

_____

_____

_____

_____

Question: How can you naturally share the gospel?

_____

_____

_____

_____

_____

_____

_____

_____

_____

_____

Action: Don't let fear, arrogance, ignorance, or apathy keep you from answering God's call and requirement to share the gospel of Jesus Christ. Make sure you share the true message of salvation—of repentance and God's saving grace through the cross. Share it naturally, listening first, and don't think of evangelism simply as a sales pitch.

Chapter 3 Notes

_____

_____

_____

_____

_____

_____

_____

_____

_____

_____

_____

_____

_____

_____

_____

_____

_____

_____

_____

_____

_____

_____

_____

_____

CHAPTER FOUR

Discipleship: The Cost of Delivering the Message

When Christ calls a man, he bids him to come and die.—
Dietrich Bonhoeffer[14]

Jesus made it clear we must not only share the good news of the gospel of Christ with others, but we must also lead people to grow spiritually. We must model and instruct them in how to live in obedience to God's Word and to follow Him. This is called "discipleship," and should be the natural byproduct of those who follow Jesus.

Learning to Bear Our Cross

The call that Jesus gave was a call to follow Him, a call to submission, and a call to obedience. It was never a plea to make some kind of momentary decision to acquire forgiveness and peace and heaven and then go on living any way you wanted. The invitations of Jesus to the lost were always direct calls to a costly commitment. — **John MacArthur**[15]

The word "disciple" has been defined as a "learner or student." However, discipleship is more than that. Being a disciple is folfurthlowing and committing to adhere to another person's teachings. This involves acceptance of the teacher's views and practices. In other words, it means learning with the purpose to obey what is learned. It involves a deliberate choice, a definite denial, and determined obedience. The Pharisees, for example, prided themselves in being disciples of Moses (John 9:28).

Jesus's followers were called disciples. Their discipleship began with Jesus's call and required them to exercise their will in response (Matthew 9:9). The same goes for Christians today. Anyone who has committed to Jesus Christ and His teachings is also His disciple.

A disciple of Jesus Christ, then, is a pupil who accepts His teachings not only in belief but also in lifestyle. However, there is a cost for those who place themselves at their Master's disposal. Let's look at what the Bible has to say about discipleship:

> Now great crowds accompanied him, and he turned and said to them, "If anyone comes to me and does not hate his own father and mother and wife and children and brothers and sisters, yes, and even his own life, he cannot be my disciple. Whoever does not bear his own cross and come after me cannot be my disciple. For which of you, desiring to build a tower, does not first sit down and count the cost, whether he has enough to complete it? Otherwise, when he has laid a foundation and is not able to finish, all who see

it begin to mock him, saying, 'This man began to build and was not able to finish.' Or what king, going out to encounter another king in war, will not sit down first and deliberate whether he is able with ten thousand to meet him who comes against him with twenty thousand? And if not, while the other is yet a great way off, he sends a delegation and asks for terms of peace. So therefore, any one of you who does not renounce all that he has cannot be my disciple..."— Luke 14: 25-33 (ESV)

Jesus was clear about what the road would be like for the disciple in Luke 14:25-33. In this passage, Jesus was teaching great crowds who were not necessarily His disciples yet. Jesus spelled out for those listening the requirements for anyone who would answer the call to be His disciple.

First, Jesus taught that no one could be His disciple unless they loved Him more than their family (Luke 14:26). He also taught that no one could be His disciple unless they loved him more than their own self—even their own life (Luke 14:27). Finally, a person could not be Jesus's disciple unless they renounced everything they had to follow Him (Luke 14:28). Those are tough requirements.

Martin Luther, the father of the Protestant Reformation, said, "Religion that gives nothing, costs nothing, and suffers nothing, is worth nothing."[16] This was not new information, for Jesus had already made this clear while here on earth, saying, "Whoever does not bear his own cross and come after me cannot be my disciple" (Luke 14:27 ESV). Following Jesus will cost energy, time, patience, humility, and love. For some, following Jesus will cost their life. The question is, who will say "Yes!" to Jesus's call to "Follow me"?

The Lord Jesus came into this world with the will to give His life for it. Jesus had exactly the same will and compassion every day of His life and work as He did the day He hung on the cross. We are told in Luke 19:41, "He beheld the city, and wept over it." When our mind is allowed to crowd out the lost, our compassion to see them won will melt. The obvious way to keep a compassionate heart is to stay in close fellowship with Christ.

Bible teacher John MacArthur wrote, "I believe that every Christian is a disciple; every Christian is a follower of Christ. Some of us are following more faithfully than others, but every true believer has committed himself or herself to follow Jesus Christ."[17] The Great Commission is to preach the death and resurrection of Jesus, but then to move people toward an intimate relationship with God.

This is the call on the believer's life, and it is an issue of obedience. Puritan William Perkins wrote, "A true disciple loves, a true disciple obeys. We don't love perfectly, we don't obey perfectly. Sometimes we love very imperfectly and disobey, but the pattern of life is obedience and love for the Lord."[18]

Toward Maturity in Christ

God created us for this: to live our lives in a way that makes him look more like the greatness and the beauty and the infinite worth that he really is. — **John Piper**[19]

Discipleship starts with God. Discipleship is moving people toward maturity in Christ with the goal of encouraging Christ-like character and reproduction, which then leads to discipling others. It is the process of a believer's transformation that changes them to be increasingly more like Jesus. This can only be accomplished through the Word of God and the power of the Holy Spirit within an environment of loving accountability.

Paul told Timothy, "The things you have heard me say in the presence of many witnesses entrust to reliable people who will also be qualified to teach others" (2 Timothy 2:2 NIV). This is the model Christ left us with. As Paul taught his disciples to "Follow my example, as I follow the example of Christ" (1 Corinthians 11:1 NIV), so must we teach others to do the same.

As this process continues, every believer in the chain continues the work of discipleship. It should involve fellowship, ministry and mission experiences, and worship.

Fellowship

Part of discipling others should involve connecting people with other Christians in the local church so their faith might be further built up. This is called fellowship, an English word that comes from the Greek word *koinonia*. The root of this word was connected to such words as family, home, and meeting. Thus, Christian fellowship, according to the Bible, is the mutually beneficial relationship between brothers and sisters in Christ meeting as a family. This relationship simply is not possible with people outside the faith. God enabled this type of fellowship by His grace as a blessing to those who follow Him, knowing that the road would not be easy. The writer of Hebrews expresses the importance of fellowship with other believers: "Not forsaking the assembling of ourselves together, as the manner of some is; but exhorting one another: and so much the more, as ye see the day approaching" (Hebrews 10:25).

Neil T. Anderson wrote:

> Aloneness can lead to loneliness. God's preventative for loneliness is intimacy—meaningful, open, sharing relationships with one another. In Christ, we have the capacity for the fulfilling sense of belonging which comes from intimate fellowship with God and with other believers.[20]

As we grow closer to the Lord's return, the necessity of meeting together will be paramount. God's desire is that His body be one, unified, and operating as one—and it is for a great purpose: "so that the world may know that you sent me" (John 17:23 ESV). When the body of Christ is unified, the witness will bring the world toward saving faith.

Ultimately, we should be fellowshipping with other believers, because this is imitating Christ and the fellowship we have with Him: "God is faithful, by whom you were called into the fellowship of his Son, Jesus Christ our Lord" (1 Corinthians 1:9 ESV).

Ministry and Missions

In addition to encouraging fellowship with other believers, part of discipling another is helping them to find their place in ministry and missions by discovering their spiritual gifts and then using them to edify the body of Christ.

Scripture reveals that God has given each person who has trusted in Him spiritual gifts to be used to build others up. 1 Peter 4:10 (ESV) says, "As each has received a gift, use it to serve one another, as good stewards of God's varied grace" (1 Peter 4:10 ESV). Once a person has believed Christ, it is important that they understand that their response to this new freedom in Christ should be to serve one another.

For you were called to freedom, brothers. Only do not use your freedom as an opportunity for the flesh, but through love serve one another. For the whole law is fulfilled in one word: "You shall love your neighbor as yourself."— **Galatians 5:13-14 (ESV)**

There are many different gifts listed in Scripture. The goal when discipling is to help newer Christians discern what gifts God has given them. The verses below list some of the many gifts that the Holy Spirit gives to God's people.

Having then gifts differing according to the grace that is given to us, whether prophecy, let us prophesy according to the proportion of faith; Or ministry, let us wait on our ministering: or he that teacheth, on teaching; Or he that exhorteth, on exhortation: he that giveth, let him do it with simplicity; he that ruleth, with diligence; he that sheweth mercy, with cheerfulness. — **Romans 12:6-8**

Now there are diversities of gifts, but the same Spirit. And there are differences of administrations, but the same Lord. And there are diversities of operations, but it is the same God which worketh all in all. But the manifestation of the Spirit is given to every man to profit withal. For to one is given by the Spirit the word of wisdom; to another the word of knowledge by the same Spirit; To another faith by the same Spirit; to another the gifts of healing by the same Spirit; To another the working of miracles; to another prophecy; to another discerning of spirits; to another divers kinds of tongues; to another the interpretation of tongues: But all these worketh that one and the selfsame Spirit, dividing to every man severally as he will. — **1 Corinthians 12:4-11**

Nancy Ortberghas said that every spiritual gift gives off clues. She wrote:

Your spiritual gift will cause you to react a certain way in a given situation. If there's a problem, people with the spiritual gift of shepherding will be immediately concerned that people are cared for and growing in Christlikeness as a result of the issue. Those with the gift of intercession—prayer—will immediately say, "We need to pray about this," while those with a leadership gift will begin looking at solutions for the problem.[21]

Believers should be helping others identify how they might be gifted and best serve the body of Christ.

Worship

Furthermore, discipling should involve leading people to express their adoration and love for God. This is called worship. Though the Bible doesn't give an official definition of worship, in English, the word comes from two Old English words: *weoth,* which means worth, and *-ship* which means quality. Certain English words today have that -ship ending, such as friendship. Thus, friendship means the quality of being a friend.

Thus, *worth-ship* or worship means having worth or being worthy. When we worship God, we are honoring Him as being worthy above everything on earth, under the earth, and in heaven. Peter wrote about worshipping God, saying, "But ye are a chosen generation, a royal priesthood, an holy nation, a peculiar people; that *ye should shew forth the praises of him who hath called you out of darkness into his marvelous light...* (1 Peter 2:9, emphasis added).

Worship is more than singing praises, as modern church services often reflect—although worship absolutely occurs through song. Worship involves speaking, listening, and doing for God's glory. It expresses the heart of the worshipper toward God—a response to God of gratefulness for what has been freely given to them by God's grace. Theologian A. W. Tozer expresses his reason for worshipping God in these words:

Sometimes I go to God and say, "God, if Thou dost never answer another prayer while I live on this earth, I will still worship Thee as long as I live and in the ages to come for what Thou hast done already." God's already put me so far in debt that if I were to live one million millennia I couldn't pay Him for what He's done for me.[22]

Both the Old Testament and the New Testament indicate that our worship should involve a person's heart, mind, and soul. When asked what the greatest commandment was, Jesus answered by quoting Deuteronomy 6: "Thou shalt love the LORD thy God with all thy heart, and with all thy soul, and with all thy strength, and with all thy mind; and thy neighbour as thyself" (Luke 10:27).

This is the heart of worship: Loving God and acknowledging Him as the incomprehensible God that He is, and loving others.

Jesus as Our Model Soul-Winner

The one who says he abides in Him ought himself to walk in the same manner as He walked. — 1 John 2:6 (NASB)

A disciple should be a soul-winning follower of Jesus, because the world needs courageous disciples committed to helping people grow. All people—regardless of ethnicity, religion, or even political stance—are a part of the world Jesus came to save, and therefore, part of our responsibility to reach them for Christ.

Therefore, part of the cost of discipleship is a never-ending, full-on, life-transforming evangelism, as explained in chapter two. Anyone who follows Jesus must learn how to imitate Him and be able to participate in conversations—naturally turning them in a spiritual direction that provides opportunities for sharing one's faith. You must learn how to become a contagious Christian who makes a difference in others' lives.

It takes persistence to draw others close without overpowering the conversation, but we should feel obligated both to share the faith and to help those newer Christians around us. In this era, you can become a soul-winning disciple not only because there is a world around you in need, but also because there is a will. God has a will for you to become a soul-winning disciple. Jesus has a will for the same. Those who have answered Jesus's call have the same will, because the Lord dwells within them.

Jesus Himself was a personal soul-winner, a model disciple-maker, and the perfect example for us to follow when reaching out to others to share the good news of the gospel. Everywhere Jesus went, He was winning souls.

One night, a Jewish Pharisee met Jesus privately at dusk. He knew in his soul there was something different about this man Jesus—even though he was a Pharisee and Pharisees were standing in great opposition to Jesus and His teachings. That night, Nicodemus's life changed. Jesus told Nicodemus that in order to see the kingdom of God, a person needed to be born again (John 3:3). Nicodemus was confused and questioned this, saying,

"How can a man be born when he is old? Can he enter a second time into his mother's womb, and be born?"

Jesus's response is the linchpin to salvation, and a model for us to follow: "Verily, verily, I say unto thee, Except a man be born of water and of the Spirit, he cannot enter into the kingdom of God" (John 3:5). Salvation did not occur for Nicodemus by something physical or external being done to him, or by him doing any good work himself. Salvation occurs at the moment of belief when a person is born of the Spirit.

Many other examples throughout Scripture support this. In an intimate conversation with the woman at the well, Jesus told her, "God is a Spirit: and they that worship him must worship him in spirit and in truth (John 4:24).

Jesus indicated salvation was an internal change that would be reflected to those who would see that change. After healing a blind man, Jesus said He had performed the miracle "that the works of God should be made manifest in him" (John 9:30).

Zacchaeus, a man short of stature and a dishonest tax collector, had climbed up into a tree to see this Jesus. When Jesus beckoned him to come down—for He wanted to share a meal with him—Zacchaeus repented of his sinful ways. Jesus said: "This day is salvation come to this house, forasmuch as he also is a son of Abraham. For the Son of man is come to seek and to save that which was lost" (Luke 19:9-10). Zacchaeus had not been baptized at that moment in time, and yet Jesus said that very day Zacchaeus was saved.

Finally, as Jesus was hanging on the cross nearing death, he extended salvation to one of the thieves next to him—simply because the thief asked for forgiveness of his sin. After the thief confessed his sin, Jesus said him, "Verily I say unto thee, Today shalt thou be with me in paradise" (Luke 23:43).

If you follow and watch Jesus, you'll discover that He was always doing the work of soul-winning—up to the moment of His death.

The Attitude of Christ

Those who follow Him lead by example. They never make a grand entrance; they come in through the service door. —
D. J. De Haan[23]

Jesus was winning souls not only by healing people, but also by serving others. Paul recognized the importance of imitating Christ, saying, "Be ye followers of me, even as I also am of Christ" (1 Corinthians 11:1).

Paul also wrote that the disciple should do this by imitating Christ's attitude (Philippians 2:5), which was one of humility. Though Jesus was "in the form of God, thought it not robbery to be equal with God: But made himself of no reputation, and took upon him the form of a servant, and was made in the likeness of men..." (Philippians 2:6-7). Jesus did not consider His equality with God something to be held onto at the cost of our eternal separation from Him. Instead, He made Himself nothing, in the "likeness of men," to save us.

On July 20, 1969, Apollo 11 astronauts landed on the moon. It was an unprecedented human achievement. Millions remember the words of Neil Armstrong: "That's one small step for man, one giant leap for mankind." President Nixon declared, "All humanity is one in their pride."

Two thousand years earlier, the One who created the moon in the first place descended from heaven to earth (Philippians 2:5-8)—a leap of a miraculous kind. Jesus, the eternal Word (John 1:1, 14) stepped down from heaven to become fully human while remaining fully God. It was an amazing leap—the ultimate act of revealing God's heart of love for His people. He became one of us so He could die on the cross to pay the penalty for our sins. Through His life and death, sin was forgiven; those who receive Him receive His Spirit, which enables us to overcome selfish motives and a prideful heart, and to be able to love others as He did (Philippians 2:3-4).

Jesus showed this love in action when washing the disciple's feet in John 13. With a towel around his waist, Jesus cleaned the dirt off the feet of His motley crew of disciples, showing them what it means to truly disciple others. What love! And what a model for us to follow.

In coming to this earth, Jesus became part of a long-running play, but He was not acting. He took the servant part for some thirty-three years to show people how to live (Philippians 2:7). This might seem backward to a world that is me-focused, and bent on seeking the self first. Jesus's example of true discipleship was dying to the self for the benefit and love of others. Discipling this way will open the door to natural conversations that can be gently steered toward spiritual truths, and ultimately, the message of salvation by faith can be shared.

Chapter 4 Questions

Question: What does your identity as a disciple of Jesus mean to you? How can you fulfill this identity more completely?

_____

_____

_____

_____

_____

_____

_____

_____

_____

_____

Question: What are the main elements or aspects of discipleship and spiritual maturity? Which areas do you need to strengthen in your own discipleship, and how will you do so?

_____

_____

_____

_____

_____

_____

_____

_____

_____

_____

Question: What does it mean to follow the model of Christ in winning souls? How exactly will you put this into practice?

_____

_____

_____

_____

_____

_____

_____

_____

_____

_____

_____

Action: As God's saving grace transforms your life, train your heart to follow Jesus's example of love, humility, and service. Develop your spiritual maturity in the areas of fellowship, ministry and missions, and worship, as well as in evangelism. Then model yourself after Christ in winning souls as you carry the cross of discipleship daily and become a contagious Christian!

Chapter 4 Notes

CONCLUSION

Answering the Call

This is the call of God on your life.

In the beginning was the Word, and the Word was with God, and the Word was God. He was with God in the beginning. All things were created through Him, and apart from Him not one thing was created that has been created. Life was in Him, and that life was the light of men. That light shines in the darkness, yet the darkness did not overcome it.— **John 1:1-5 (HCSB)**

One of the main reasons people don't answer the call is because they do not trust. Trusting Jesus means turning toward God and away from selfish, prideful living. Listening to His Word, experiencing His miracles, going to church, and praying is not enough. Every person must make the choice to turn from sin and trust in the forgiveness and salvation that are only available through Jesus. Trusting in Jesus Christ is the first step not only in developing a lifelong relationship with the Savior of the world, but also in fulfilling Jesus's commandment to go, teach, and baptize in His name.

Moreover, as the famous theologian Matthew Henry wrote: "Christians must be of Christ's mind. We must bear a resemblance to His life if we would have the benefit of His death."[24] Paul likewise wrote that "you are not in the flesh but in the Spirit, if indeed the Spirit of God dwells in you. But if anyone does not have the Spirit of Christ, he does not belong to Him" (Romans 8:9 NASB).

Ultimately, if we are to get back to the message of the gospel and make a difference in this new era, we must be of one mind and spirit with Christ. Answering Jesus's call requires us to train our hearts and our daily practice of faith in Him, His Word, and His perfect model of soul-winning discipleship.

REFERENCES

Notes

1. Spurgeon, Charles. "A Defense of Calvinism." *The Spurgeon Archive.* http://www.spurgeon.org/calvinis.php
2. Holladay, William. *A Concise Hebrew and Aramaic Lexicon of the Old Testament.* William B. Eerdmans, 1972.
3. Williams, Michael D. *Far As the Curse Is Found: The Covenant Story of Redemption.* P & R, 2005.
4. Boyd, Nathaniel, Sr. *The Informer.* http://www.iahe.net/informer
5. Martin, David. "Common Sense Questions a 'Church of Christ' Preacher Cannot Answer." http://www.biblebelievers.com/david_martin/martin_church-christ.html
6. Holladay, Tom. *Foundations Participant's Guide: A Purpose-Driven Discipleship Resource—11 Core Truths to Build Your Life.* Zondervan, 2003.

7. Chambers, Oswald. "Not by Might nor by Power." *My Utmost for His Highest.* http://utmost.org/not-by-might-nor-by-power/

8. *Webster's New World College Dictionary*, s.v. "Faith." http://www.yourdictionary.com/faith#websters

9. Carmichael, Amy. "Amy Carmichael Quotes." *Goodreads.com.* Goodreads. http://www.goodreads.com/author/quotes/393588 1.Amy_Carmichael

10. Reagan, David.

11. Spurgeon, Charles. *Good News Toolbox.* http://www.goodnewstoolbox.com/index.php?opt ion=com_content&view=article&id=3:as-soon-as&catid=2:top-lhs-quotes

12. Piper, John. "In 'God's Family.'" *Vineyard Christian Fellowship.* http://new.vcfbellefontaine.org/sermon/gods-family/

13. MacArthur, John. "Inspirational Bible Verses about Evangelism," in *What Christians Want to Know. Telling Ministries.* http://www.whatchristianswanttoknow.com/inspi rational-bible-verses-about-evangelism/

14. Bonhoeffer, Dietrich. *The Cost of Discipleship.* Touchstone, 1995.

15. MacArthur, John. "The Cost of Discipleship," in *Grace To You.* Grace Community Church, 1988. http://www.gty.org/resources/sermons/90-23/the-cost-of-discipleship

16. Luther, Martin. "Religion Quotes." *Tentmaker.* Tentmaker Ministries, 2015. http://www.tentmaker.org/Quotes/religionquotes. htm

17. MacArthur, John. "The Cost of Discipleship," in *Grace To You.* Grace Community Church, 1988. http://www.gty.org/resources/sermons/90-23/the-cost-of-discipleship

18. Perkins, William. "The Cost of Discipleship," in *Grace To You.* Grace Community Church, 1988. http://www.gty.org/resources/sermons/90-23/the-cost-of-discipleship

19. Piper, John. "John Piper Quotes." *Goodreads.* http://www.goodreads.com/quotes/242097-god-created-us-for-this-to-live-our-lives-in

20. Anderson, Neil T. "Neil T. Anderson." *Daily Christian Quotes.* Katherine Walden, 2002. http://www.dailychristianquote.com/neil-t-anderson-3/

21. Ortberg, Nancy. "How Do I Uncover My Spiritual Gifts?" *Christianity Today.* http://www.todayschristianwoman.com/articles/2 007/january/how-do-i-uncover-my-spiritual-gifts.html

22. Tozer, A. W. "A. W. Tozer Quotes." *Goodreads.* http://www.goodreads.com/quotes/179057-sometimes-i-go-to-god-and-say-god-if-thou

23. De Haan, D. J. "Philippians Illustrations 2: Philippians 2," in *Precept Austin.* http://preceptaustin.org/philippians_illustrations_2.htm

24. Henry, Matthew. "Philippians 2." *Matthew Henry Commentary on the Whole Bible*. Bible Study Tools. http://www.biblestudytools.com/commentaries/matthew-henry-complete/philippians/2.html

About the Author

Dr. Mario A. Elcock is a native of Central America who grew up in Brooklyn, New York. He has resided in Indianapolis, Indiana and is the proud Senior Pastor of Mount Nebo Missionary Baptist Church. He accepted his call to preach the gospel in 1998 and was ordained in September 2002. Mario is very supportive of the church; kingdom-building through the Word of God is his passion. He earned his Masters and Doctorate degree from North Carolina College of Theology. He is a certified instructor of the National Baptist Convention, USA.

He received his certification as a chaplain with IU/Riley Hospital in May of 2014. He is also a board member of Life Touch Health Care, Indianapolis, IN.

Because of his love for God and his commitment to his fellow yoked men of the gospel, God gave him a vision to establish Under Construction Ministries as the Founder and CEO. Under Construction Ministries provides biblical instruction for men and women who have accepted the call to preach the gospel and are in leadership positions.

Mario is the husband of Dr. Lardie Elcock and they share five children.

"Now unto Him that is able to keep you from falling, and to present you faultless, before the present of His glory, with exceeding joy" (Jude 1:24).

About Sermon to Book

SermonToBook.com began with a simple belief: that sermons should be touching lives, *not* collecting dust. That's why we turn sermons into high-quality books that are accessible to people all over the globe.

Turning your sermon series into a book exposes more people to God's Word, better equips you for counseling, accelerates future sermon prep, adds credibility to your ministry, and even helps make ends meet during tight times.

John 21:25 tells us that the world itself couldn't contain the books that would be written about the work of Jesus Christ. Our mission is to try anyway. Because, in heaven, there will no longer be a need for sermons or books. Our time is now.

If God so leads you, we'd love to work with you on your sermon or sermon series.

Visit www.sermontobook.com to learn more.

www.ingramcontent.com/pod-product-compliance
Lightning Source LLC
LaVergne TN
LVHW051425080426
835508LV00022B/3249